The Gamble

Based on the television series created by Josh Schwartz including the episode 'The Model Home', story by Allan Heinberg & Josh Schwartz and written by Josh Schwartz; the episode 'The Gamble', written by Jane Espenson; and the episode 'The Debut', written by Allan Heinberg & Josh Schwartz

LEVEL 3

■SCHOLASTIC

Adapted by: Patricia Reilly
Fact Files written by: Jacquie Bloese
Commissioning Editor: Jacquie Bloese
Editor: Fiona Davis
Designer: Dawn Wilson
Picture research: Emma Bree
Photo credits:
Cover and inside images courtesy of Warner Bros.
Page 60: A. Hussein/Empics; Stockhause.
Page 61: R. Van Der Hilst/Corbis; Stockhause.

 Copyright © 2007 Warner Bros. Entertainment Inc.
THE O.C. and all related characters and elements are trademarks of and © Warner Bros. Entertainment Inc.
WB SHIELD: ™ & © Warner Bros. Entertainment Inc.
MARY 6532

Fact File text and design © Scholastic Ltd. 2007
All rights reserved.

Published by Scholastic Ltd.

No part of this publication may be reproduced in whole or in part, or stored in a retrieval system, or transmitted in any form or by any means, electronic, mechanical, photocopying, recording or otherwise, without written permission of the publisher. For information regarding permission write to:

Mary Glasgow Magazines (Scholastic Ltd.)
Euston House
24 Eversholt Street
London NW1 1DB

Printed in Singapore. Reprinted in 2009.
This edition printed in 2011.

Contents

	Page
The Gamble	**4–55**
People and places	**4–5**
The story so far	**6**
Chapter 1: Seth's plan	**7**
Chapter 2: The fight	**13**
Chapter 3: The fire	**18**
Chapter 4: A surprise visitor	**24**
Chapter 5: Vegas Night	**30**
Chapter 6: 'Two handsome young men …'	**38**
Chapter 7: Dancing, not fighting	**41**
Chapter 8: Dance partners	**46**
Chapter 9: The debutante dance	**50**
Fact Files	**56–61**
On set with *The OC*	**56**
Mischa Barton	**58**
Debutante balls	**60**
Self-Study Activities	**62–64**
New Words!	**inside back cover**

PEOPLE AND PLACES

LUKE WARD
Luke is Marissa's boyfriend. He's everything a guy from Newport should be: rich, popular and good-looking.
Secret? Marissa isn't his only girlfriend ...

DAWN ATWOOD
Ryan's mom, but nobody knows where she is.
Secret? She loves her kids but she drinks too much.

RYAN ATWOOD
Ryan is from Chino, but he's living with the Cohens in Newport.
Secrets? He's been in prison, and he likes Marissa ... really likes her.

SANDY & KIRSTEN COHEN
Seth's mom and dad. Sandy invited Ryan to stay, and Kirsten wasn't happy about it.
Secrets? None. They seem to be the perfect couple.

MARISSA COOPER
Marissa is bored with her life. Luke's always been her boyfriend. Now Ryan's arrived and she doesn't know what she wants.
Secrets? She's worried about her dad. Oh, and sometimes she drinks too much.

ANNA STERN
Anna has just arrived in Newport – she's from Pittsburg. She's funny, clever and beautiful.
Secrets? There's still everything to learn about Anna.

PLACES

Newport Beach Welcome to California – and this rich town by the sea. Here you'll find lots of rich kids, big houses and expensive cars.
Chino It's still California and only an hour away from Newport Beach, but life is a lot harder here.

JIMMY & JULIE COOPER
Marissa's mom and dad.
Secrets? Jimmy's having big problems at work, but Julie doesn't know.

SETH COHEN
Seth lives in Newport Beach, next door to Marissa.
Secrets? He's been in love with Summer for years, but she doesn't know. He hates Newport and he thinks no one there likes him.

SUMMER ROBERTS
Summer is Marissa's best friend.
Secret? She seems to choose the wrong guys! She hasn't even noticed Seth … yet.

The story so far

Hey, Trey!

Hey, big brother, how are you?

Why did we steal that car? It was so stupid. I got probation, but when I got home, Mom told me to leave. Can you believe it? I didn't have anywhere to go, so I phoned Sandy Cohen, my attorney. He's OK. Anyway, he took me to his home in Newport.

Newport's not like Chino. You should see the houses and cars! Everyone is so rich! I had to sleep in the Cohens' pool house because Kirsten, Sandy's wife, didn't want me in the house.

Sandy and Kirsten have a son, Seth. He's sixteen too. The other kids think he's a geek, but he's cool really. Oh, and I met this girl, Marissa. She lives next door and, wow, she's beautiful! She's got this stupid boyfriend, Luke.

Summer, Marissa's best friend, invited me to a party with all the rich kids. It was wild. Luke and his friends started a fight with me and Seth. Marissa got really drunk and Luke disappeared with another girl. Seth and I came back and then I found Marissa drunk outside her house. Her friends had just left her there! I took her back to the pool house but when I woke up, she wasn't there.

Kirsten found out about the fight and she was really angry. She asked me to leave. Sandy drove me back to Chino. Marissa saw us leave Newport, but we didn't get a chance to speak. When we got to Chino, the house was empty. Mom had gone. She just left a note!

I'm back in Newport with Sandy now. I don't know what's going to happen next …

Have to go now, dude – I'll try and write again soon.

Ryan

CHAPTER 1
Seth's plan

'Number 038-29-65,' Ryan thought as he looked at the paper in his hand. 'That's all I am now – a number. I haven't got a family – Dad and Trey are in prison and Mom's disappeared. And I can't stay with the Cohens. What's going to happen to me?'

Ryan was in the kitchen with Sandy, Kirsten and Seth. He didn't want to sign the paper.

'Look, it just says that you don't have a parent or guardian,' Sandy explained. 'That's all.'

Ryan signed.

'Tomorrow we'll go to the group home*,' Sandy continued. 'I've got you a room with only two other kids. Sometimes they can be crowded ...'

Ryan looked at him. Sandy was trying to make him feel better, but it wasn't helping. A group home sounded horrible.

Sandy knew Ryan wasn't happy. 'Look,' he said, 'they could find you a home with a family.'

'Yeah, right,' Seth said, 'because *everyone* wants a sixteen-year-old guy.'

'Seth!' his parents said. But Seth didn't care – he was upset. Ryan was his first real friend and now his parents wanted Ryan to leave. He'd never see him again. 'We have all this space *and* a pool house, and you want him to go to a group home?' Seth stopped. 'Am I the only one who thinks that's crazy?'

Ryan was stunned. Seth was a real friend. 'It's OK, Seth,' he said. 'Really.'

* A group home is a place where children with no parents or guardians live together.

Ryan looked at the model home* which Kirsten had brought home from work. Kirsten worked for her father. His company built most of the big houses in Newport. The model was beautiful. Ryan tried to imagine living in a house like that – with a family and parents who loved him.

'Good luck with it. It looks perfect,' he said to Kirsten.

Then he went out to the pool house.

***

Seth was almost at the pool house when the door suddenly opened.

'Hey, I saw your light and …' Seth saw Ryan's bag. 'You're running away? What about the group home?'

'I don't want to live in a group home,' Ryan said angrily.

'I'll come with you.'

'No,' said Ryan. He had to do this by himself.

'But what are you going to do?' asked Seth.

Ryan looked away. 'I don't know. Leave town. Get a job somewhere …'

'Great plan, dude. I can see you've really thought about it.'

'Have you got a better idea?' asked Ryan.

---

* A small copy of a building.

'Yeah,' said Seth, 'I have.'

Ryan looked at him and thought for a moment. 'OK …
I'll wait for you down by the road, but be quick!'

Ten minutes later, Ryan was still waiting. Where *was*
Seth? Suddenly Marissa walked out of her house and saw
Ryan. She looked surprised.

'I … thought you'd left,' she said finally. She wanted to
say more, but instead she just stood there.

'I had to come back …'

Just then, Seth came up carrying his skateboard and a
bag. He saw Marissa and stopped.

Marissa looked at Seth and his bag, and Ryan and his
bag.

'What are you guys planning?' she asked.

'Nothing,' Seth said.

'You should go,' Ryan said. But Marissa wasn't leaving.
She wanted to be part of the plan – and she had a car.

***

'So … what music do you like?' They were in the car
and Marissa was trying to find out more about Ryan.

'Everything … I don't know … I don't really listen to
music,' Ryan said.

Ryan realised Marissa and Seth were looking at him in
surprise.

'What do you listen to?' he asked Marissa.

'Punk. I love *The Clash*, *Sex Pistols*, *The Cramps* …'

'No!' cried Seth from the back of the car. 'I like the same
music as Marissa Cooper. I may have to kill myself!'

'Why punk?' Ryan asked Marissa.

'I'm angry,' she replied.

Ryan liked that.

***

'So what do you think?' Seth asked. They were standing in front of an unfinished house.

Suddenly Ryan realised where they were. 'It's your mom's model home!' he said as they went inside.

'You can stay as long as you want – until we have a real plan. And *that* …' Seth pointed outside, 'is the best bit.'

'Seth, it's an empty pool,' Ryan said.

'Some people might think so,' said Seth. And he disappeared.

Ryan and Marissa went outside and sat by the empty pool.

'So …' Ryan started.

'So …' Marissa replied. They fell silent.

'Why *did* you come back?' Marissa asked suddenly.

'I went back to Chino, but the house was empty. My mom had left,' Ryan said.

Marissa felt bad. They were silent again.

Seth came back on his skateboard. 'Did you miss me?'

Ryan and Marissa smiled. Seth started skateboarding round the pool.

'But your mom … she's coming back, right?' Marissa asked.

'I don't know.'

'Well, what about your dad? Can you call him?' she said.

'My dad's in prison,' Ryan said.

Marissa didn't know what to say. 'My dad works for a company, but I think he's in trouble,' she said finally. 'He's stopped going to the office and these guys came to the house. They were police, I think. I … I haven't told anyone.'

'Maybe that's why she gets drunk,' Ryan thought. 'I can keep a secret,' he said.

Marissa's phone rang. It was Luke. He was waiting for her at a party at Holly's house.

Ryan thought about Holly's last party. Marissa had got very drunk and Luke had disappeared with another girl. He wanted to tell her, but he couldn't.

Marissa finished talking to Luke and turned to Ryan and Seth.

'Hey, guys – I have to go soon.'

They all went back into the house.

'How long have you and Luke been together?' Ryan asked.

'Those two?' said Seth. 'They've been together for years and years.'

'What's your problem, Cohen? What did I ever do to you?' Marissa said.

'Nothing,' Seth smiled. 'I've lived next door to you all my life and you've never done or said anything to me.'

'But *you* never talk to *me*,' Marissa cried. 'You think you're so much better than everyone else.'

Seth was stunned. Marissa thought *he* didn't want to talk to *her*? For years he'd thought the other kids didn't want to talk to *him*.

Ryan looked around him. 'Maybe it's not a good idea for me to stay,' he said.

Marissa smiled at him. 'You should stay,' she said. Her phone rang again.

'Was that Summer?' asked Seth excitedly when Marissa finished talking.

'Yeah … I've got to meet my friends,' Marissa said. She smiled at them both. 'My *other* friends …'

The three of them stood silent for a moment. In just one night they had become friends.

***

Seth's parents were asleep when he got home. He walked through the house as quietly as he could. His plan was a success. He had hidden Ryan and they didn't know. He got into bed and smiled. 'It was worth it,' he thought.

***

Marissa was at Holly's party, but she wasn't enjoying it. She looked around the room. She realised that she only had fun with these people when she was drinking. They always did the same thing, talked about the same people. Every night. And she was bored. She didn't even want to talk to Luke. She decided to leave.

Back home, she started thinking about Ryan. 'How would it feel to kiss him?' she wondered. She put on some music but it didn't stop her thinking about him. 'I'll make a CD for Ryan,' she thought. 'And call it 'The Model Home Mix'.'

***

Lying on the hard floor in the model home, Ryan couldn't sleep. Thoughts raced around his head. Marissa. His mom. 'Will I ever have a home and a family again?' he wondered.

CHAPTER 2
The fight

'Come on!' Ryan said as he rode over to Marissa.

She climbed onto the back of his bike and held his shoulders. They rode past all the beach houses with Seth following on his skateboard. Soon they reached the beach.

'Hurry up!' Marissa pretended she wanted to go faster. She could see Luke surfing in the water. She didn't want Luke to see her with Ryan. She felt like she was cheating on Luke. But part of her didn't care – when she was with Ryan she felt free and she liked it.

As they raced down to the pier, Marissa covered Ryan's eyes with her hands. Ryan tried not to fall off. By the time they reached the diner, they were all laughing. None of them had had so much fun for a long time.

'Thanks for the ride,' Marissa laughed.

'Any time. And thanks for 'The Model Home Mix',' Ryan said.

'It'll help you to survive life in Newport …' Marissa laughed again.

'See, this could be the first place in our tour of the country,' Seth said as they sat in the diner eating their food.

'Like in *On the Road**? That's my favourite book,' said Marissa

'Mine too.' Seth was surprised. 'First Marissa likes the same music as me, and now we have the same favourite book! I don't believe it,' he thought.

'So,' Ryan said, 'I was thinking … my mom used to have this boyfriend. He was OK. I did some work for him in a building company. He moved to Austin.'

* *On the Road* is Jack Kerouac's famous book about travelling around the USA.

'Austin in *Texas*?' Marissa didn't want Ryan to go.
'That's a long way,' Seth added.
'I've got no choice. I can't stay in the model home forever.'

'In a way you're lucky,' Seth said. 'You can go to a new place. Start again. You can be anything you want.'

'Seth's right,' Ryan thought, but he looked at Marissa and knew it would be hard to leave.

Just then, Luke and his friends, Nordlund and Saunders, walked into the diner. This was not good.

'OK, I'll talk to them,' said Marissa. 'You two go out the back before anyone sees you.'

Seth and Ryan quickly got up. Ryan watched as Marissa walked over to the group and Luke put his arm around her. He wanted to hit Luke and tell him Marissa was too good for him. But he didn't. He just watched and followed Seth to the back door. It was locked. As they turned round, a waiter with a large pile of plates crashed into Ryan. Seth jumped in front of Ryan – he didn't want Luke to see him.

'Hey, Luke! Guys!' he called. 'Do you like the food here?'

'Shut up, geek!' Luke laughed at him.

'At least I don't shave my chest … like you,' Seth said quietly.

'What did you say?' Luke shouted. He stood up. 'Do you want me to hit you, Cohen?'

Suddenly Ryan turned and looked at Luke.

'Your food's getting cold,' he said.

'Look who's back!' said Luke in surprise. 'You're a long way from Chino.'

'Luke. Come on,' Marissa was embarrassed by Luke.

'What? Are you friends with these guys now?' Luke said angrily.

'You know what I like about rich kids?' Ryan asked. Then he hit Luke. 'Nothing.'

Luke fell to the floor and Seth and Ryan ran out. Seth used his skateboard to hold the door shut. Ryan unlocked his bike and Seth jumped on the back. They soon left Luke and his friends behind.

***

Marissa sat alone at a table with her head in her hands. Luke came over.

'What's wrong?' he asked her.

'Nothing.'

'Good.' Luke kissed her. 'For a minute I thought you were worried about that geek and the Chino kid.'

'Hey, that Chino kid really hit you. Right in the stomach,' Saunders said.

'He comes back again – he's dead,' Luke said.

'You said that last time!' Nordlund laughed.

'Who asked you?' shouted Luke. He turned to Marissa and started telling her about the day's surfing. Marissa just sat in silence thinking of Ryan.

***

Seth and Ryan were back at the model home.

'Why don't you stay, Ryan? We make a good team,' said Seth.

Ryan wanted to stay, but he knew that it was impossible. He'd seen the police cars as they left the diner. If he didn't leave now, he would have to go to a group home – or worse, to Juvie* again.

Just then Marissa walked in.

'You didn't have to hit Luke,' she said.

'Yeah, he had to,' Seth said.

Ryan felt bad. 'Sorry …'

'I don't know why he's like that,' Marissa continued. 'He's just …'

'… stupid?' Seth suggested.

'… trying to protect me.' Marissa stopped. 'Hey, what's that noise?'

Seth looked out of the window. 'It's my mom's car. It's my mom … and your dad.' He looked at Marissa in surprise.

The three of them hid. Jimmy and Kirsten walked into the house. They looked very serious.

* Juvie is a prison for young (juvenile) criminals.

Marissa heard her father asking Kirsten for money. One hundred thousand dollars. She was stunned. She knew her dad was having problems ... but she didn't know things were so bad.

Ryan looked at Marissa. Maybe having a family wasn't perfect after all. But there was more bad news. The builders wanted to start work in the morning. Ryan had to leave the next day.

***

Seth was in his bedroom. He'd just bought Ryan's bus ticket to Austin on the Internet.

Sandy came into his room. 'They've found Ryan. Well, they think he was in a fight down at the pier.'

Seth tried to act cool. 'Oh, really?'

'So we should try to find him before there's any more trouble,' Sandy continued.

'What ... now?' Seth asked.

'Seth, I thought he was your friend.'

Seth knew he had to go or his dad would get suspicious. He and Sandy got into the car and started their search.

***

'So what's up? You've been acting really strangely,' Summer asked Marissa as she got another drink.

Holly was having another party at her beach house.

'Yeah? Have you ever wondered what ... what your life seems like to another person?' she asked Summer.

'See, that's *exactly* what I mean,' Summer replied. 'Strange.'

Marissa wanted to tell Summer everything – about her dad, Luke, feeling lonely and bored ... but she knew Summer wouldn't understand. Nobody understood, except Ryan. And she couldn't tell Summer about Ryan and the model home. That was secret.

CHAPTER 3
The fire

'Seriously, dude, let's find that guy,' Nordlund said to Luke and Saunders. Holly got everyone another drink.

'Who?' Summer had just arrived.

'That Chino kid. He hit Luke,' Nordlund explained.

'He's crazy,' Summer said.

'I heard that's he's totally wild,' Holly added.

'If I see him again, I'm going to kill him.' Luke was angry and a bit drunk.

Marissa walked up behind them. She'd heard everything. She was glad she hadn't told Summer anything. 'I have to go …' she said as she ran to the door.

'Hey, Marissa, wait. Where are you going?'

'I can't stay,' she said.

Luke ran after her. 'What's up?' he asked.

'You don't know him. You don't know anything about him,' Marissa said and jumped into her car.

Luke didn't know what Marissa was talking about. He watched her drive away.

***

In the model home, Ryan started to put his things in his bag. It was dark, but he'd put candles all around the room. He was listening to Marissa's CD. He looked up – and there she was.

'This song makes me think of you,' she said.

Ryan didn't move. 'I thought you were with Luke.'

'I was.'

They were both silent. Neither of them knew what to say.

'I … I don't know why I'm here,' Marissa said. 'I just wanted to see you. You're leaving tomorrow. I might never …' Marissa couldn't finish.

Ryan understood.

'Maybe I could spend the night,' Marissa whispered.

Ryan wanted to kiss her, but he didn't want to get her in trouble. 'You can't stay,' he began. 'If you stay … if we spend the night together … I don't think I could leave.'

'Then stay,' Marissa cried.

'Soon you'll go back to school. And I'll just – what? Hide in different houses until the police find me? We're from different worlds, Marissa.'

'That's not true,' she cried.

'You can't help me,' Ryan said. He didn't want to hurt her. 'Please, just go.'

Marissa started crying. She ran downstairs, out of the door and into her car. The tears were falling down her face as she drove home. Ryan ran outside after her, but it was too late.

***

Luke and his friends watched Marissa leave the model home. They had followed her. Then they saw Ryan run out.

'Hey, there's that Chino kid! What are you going to do?' asked Saunders.

'What do *you* think?' Luke glared at him.

'It's not worth it, dude. The police came before, remember?'

'Yeah, let's go back to Holly's,' Nordlund said. 'Anyway, you're cheating on her. What's the difference?'

Luke looked at Nordlund angrily. He wanted a fight.

***

Seth and Sandy were still looking for Ryan. They'd driven all around Newport, but Sandy didn't want to stop. Seth was starting to feel bad about it, but then he thought about Ryan in a group home. He said nothing and they went on looking.

***

'Seth, I'm up here. Did you get the bus ticket?' Ryan shouted when he heard someone walk upstairs.

But it wasn't Seth. It was Luke, with Nordlund and Saunders.

'Bus ticket?' said Luke. 'You're not going anywhere.'

Ryan looked at the three of them. He could see they wanted a fight. Three to one.

***

Marissa was still crying when she got home.

'Hey, Marissa,' Jimmy said.

But Marissa didn't answer. She ran up to her room and fell onto the bed.

'Marissa?' Still no answer.

Jimmy came into her room and saw her crying. 'Marissa, what's up? You can tell me,' Jimmy hugged his daughter.

'We used to talk about everything,' Marissa thought. She remembered today. The money. Kirsten. And she knew that her dad was keeping something secret.

＊＊＊

The room was quiet. Luke moved a little closer.

'What are you doing here? What are you doing with my girlfriend?' he shouted.

'Nothing.' Ryan thought about Marissa. He knew this wouldn't end well.

Luke pushed Ryan. 'It didn't look like nothing. Tell me, or I'll kill you.'

But Ryan didn't care. He was all alone.

'Kill me then.'

Luke suddenly pushed Ryan hard. Ryan kicked him and Luke shouted in pain. Ryan stepped back, but Saunders hit him and he fell to the floor. A candle fell onto Ryan's sleeping bag, but nobody noticed. The bag started burning.

Ryan stood up. Saunders was kicking and hitting him, but he got free. Then Luke was in front of him again. They were really fighting now. The blood ran down their faces. Their hate grew as the fire got bigger.

Luke threw Ryan across the room. 'What were you doing with my girlfriend?' he shouted.

Ryan's mouth hurt. He couldn't answer. Luke hit him hard in the stomach and Ryan fell to the floor. Luke kicked him and then jumped on top of him. He was really angry now. 'What were you doing here? Tell me! *Tell me*!' He hit Ryan's head hard against the floor and Ryan fell back, unconscious.

'This place is on fire! Let's go!' Nordlund shouted as he ran downstairs.

Saunders ran after him, but Luke stopped. Ryan was unconscious on the floor. Luke hated Ryan, but he couldn't just leave him there. He ran back and pulled Ryan out of the room and downstairs. Ryan's body lay on the ground, not moving.

'Let's go!' Nordlund screamed from the car. Luke ran over and jumped in. They left fast.

A few minutes later, Ryan opened his eyes and pulled himself up off the ground. He looked back. The whole house was burning. Everything he had ever owned was inside.

***

Sandy and Seth were still looking for Ryan when Kirsten phoned.

'The model home's on fire!' she told Sandy.

They drove silently to the house. By the time they arrived, the house was almost completely destroyed. Kirsten was really upset. Seth felt terrible.

'This is my fault,' Seth told his parents quietly. 'Ryan was staying here …'

***

'Was that kid still alive?' Nordlund whispered to Luke. They were back at Holly's party. Luke was looking for Marissa, but she wasn't there.

'Yeah … I think so,' Luke said.

Nordlund wasn't so sure. 'I hope so.'

Luke was starting to feel bad. He had to leave the party.

***

Ryan was walking slowly down the dark street when Luke's car stopped next to him.

'You're alive,' Luke said. He opened the car door.

Ryan thought for a moment and then got in. He knew what he had to do, and so did Luke. They drove to the Cohens' in silence.

The police were already there. Marissa was outside with the Cohens, watching. Ryan got out. He knew what would happen. He held out his hands and a police officer handcuffed him and took him to a police car. Luke slowly got out of his car. He was handcuffed and put in the car with Ryan. As they drove away, Luke couldn't look at Marissa. But Ryan kept his eyes on her, saying goodbye – maybe for the last time.

CHAPTER 4
A surprise visitor

'I couldn't just leave Ryan in Juvie ... they'd *kill* him in that place,' Kirsten was explaining to Sandy. 'He couldn't stay there. And he can't stay here. We have to find his mother.'

After the fire had destroyed the model home, Ryan had been sent to Juvie again. Kirsten and Seth had been to visit him and now he was back at the Cohens'. He stood by the kitchen door, listening.

'He doesn't want to find her,' Sandy said.

'He's a kid, Sandy. He doesn't know what he wants,' Kirsten replied.

'So I guess I'm not staying,' Ryan said quietly.

Kirsten and Sandy turned to look at him, but Ryan left the kitchen and went to the pool house.

***

The next morning, Seth and Ryan were in the pool. Ryan didn't feel like talking, but Seth had lots of questions. He wanted to know about Juvie, the fire,

Marissa, Luke …

'So what happened that night? With Marissa? Before Luke arrived,' Seth finally asked.

'She came to see me …' Ryan stopped.

'And?'

'And I told her to leave,' Ryan continued.

'You told her to leave?' Seth was stunned. 'You two are alone and you expect me to believe …'

'I thought I was leaving the next morning. It didn't seem right.' Ryan thought about Marissa. He wanted to see her, but it was better this way.

'Wow,' Seth said. 'But you're still here. And she lives next door …'

'I don't know,' Ryan said. 'I said some things. Marissa was upset.'

'Well, now you can say sorry.'

'I'm leaving soon. Maybe Luke is better for Marissa,' Ryan thought. The idea hurt.

***

Next door, Marissa was thinking exactly the opposite. She couldn't stop thinking about Ryan and she was worried about him.

'He's in Juvie, and I feel so guilty,' she thought. 'I went to see Ryan, and Luke followed me. It's all my fault – the fight and the fire.'

'Marissa. I know you're worried about that boy, but he's in Juvie now.' Julie watched as her daughter tried on another dress. 'Come on. The Vegas Charity Night is on at the club tomorrow and you must look perfect. Anyway, it's not your problem if he's in love with you.'

'He's not,' Marissa replied quickly. Too quickly.

'Why not? Does he think he's too good for you?' Julie asked.

'No, he thinks *I'm* too good for *him*.' Marissa realised it was true. 'We're from different worlds,' he had said.

'Well, he's right. And you need to think about the future. And Luke,' Julie finished.

Marissa knew her mom was right. She would never see Ryan again.

'So meet me at the club later. There's a lot to do, and I need some help.'

'OK, Mom,' Marissa agreed.

***

Later that afternoon at the club, Kirsten introduced Ryan to all the Newport women, or the 'Newpsies' as Sandy called them. The Newpsies weren't glad to meet Ryan. They knew about Luke, about the model home and about Ryan's past.

'Seth and Ryan are here to help,' Kirsten explained.

'I've heard so much about you,' Julie Cooper said to

Ryan. She wasn't friendly.

'Nice to meet you,' Ryan replied, but Julie ignored him.

Just then, Luke arrived and the Newpsies hurried over to him. Ryan was angry. Nobody cared what Luke had done. They thought it was all Ryan's fault.

Luke glared at Ryan and Ryan glared back. The room went quiet.

'I forgot Luke was coming. We can leave,' Kirsten whispered to Ryan.

'No, I'm here. I'll help.' Ryan wasn't leaving just because of Luke. He looked round the empty room.

'You big, strong guys can move all the heavy furniture. There's a lot to do,' Julie said.

***

Marissa saw Luke. He was coming through a door, carrying one end of a big table.

'Hey, your dad said you were here …' she began, but Luke ignored her. 'I thought we could talk.'

Marissa followed him. Then she realised why Luke wasn't talking. Ryan was holding the other end of the table. She was stunned. Then she felt angry. Every time she thought Ryan had left, every time she thought she had forgotten about him – he appeared again.

Luke saw Marissa looking at Ryan.

'Who do you want to talk to?' he asked angrily.

'Luke, come on,' Marissa said. But Luke dropped his end of the table and walked quickly out. Marissa looked at Ryan and took a step towards the door.

'Wait,' said Ryan. 'I feel like … since I got here I've turned your life upside-down.'

Marissa wanted to talk to Luke, but she needed to talk to Ryan too.

'I'm sorry,' she began. 'It's my fault too. It was stupid to go and see you. And those things you said …'

Now Ryan felt bad.

'But you were right,' Marissa continued. 'We're from two different worlds. It would never work. But I'm glad you're OK.'

Ryan watched Marissa leave. 'I knew it could never happen,' he thought.

***

On the drive home, Kirsten and Ryan talked. Ryan started to feel that he was part of the family.

'Maybe Kirsten will let me stay a few more days,' he thought.

But when they got home and Ryan walked into the living room, everything changed. His mom was there with Sandy.

'Hey, Ry,' she said nervously.

Ryan was stunned. He couldn't speak. 'She just disappeared and left me,' he thought angrily. He turned and left the room in silence.

***

Later that evening, the Cohens, Ryan and his mom all sat down to have dinner. No one knew what to say.

'So … Dawn,' Sandy began, 'how long have you had your new job?'

'A couple of weeks,' she answered.

'What, *another* new job? What happened this time?' Ryan asked.

Kirsten tried to change the subject. 'How's your boyfriend?'

'A.J.? We aren't together now. He hit me and Ryan …

too many times.'

Ryan was embarrassed. Dawn noticed.

'What's up? I'm saying he was no good. He drank too much.'

'Yeah, right … *A.J.* was the problem.' Ryan had heard enough. He stood up suddenly and left the room.

Dawn followed Ryan to the pool house.

'Will you at least talk to me?' Dawn shouted.

Ryan turned. 'Why are you here?'

'I came for you,' Dawn cried. But Ryan didn't believe her.

'Why? You left!' he shouted. 'You didn't even phone, you just left a note. *A note!*'

'I know, I was … And A.J. … It's going to be different now, Ryan, I promise.'

'That's what you said before – when Dad went to prison.' Ryan was still angry.

Now Dawn felt bad. 'I was too young when I married your dad and had Trey … But you … you were always the good one. When you were arrested, I didn't know what to do anymore. You were my last hope.'

Dawn started to walk to the door. Ryan didn't know what to say. He wanted to hate his mom, never see her again … but he couldn't do it. She was his family.

'Wait,' he said quietly. Then he hugged her. 'Let's just go slowly,' he said.

Dawn hugged Ryan hard. 'Whatever you want, Ry. I'm not going to lose you again …'

CHAPTER 5
Vegas Night

'So where did they go?' Seth asked Kirsten.

'I don't know. Out.'

'You just let Ryan leave with her?' Seth was worried.

'Seth, she's his mother.'

'Yeah, right. She drinks too much and she just left him. And now she comes here and you're just going to let her take Ryan away? *She* should be on probation, not Ryan,' Seth said.

Ryan and Dawn were exploring Newport. For the first time since he'd arrived there, Ryan didn't feel alone.

'This is fun,' Dawn laughed and ran down to the beach.

Ryan watched. She made him smile, and not just because she was having fun. He felt like he was part of a family again. Dawn had left him, but she had come back. And today was going well.

'Maybe we could get a flat here,' he thought.

Dawn came back and sat down next to him. 'So what do you think?' she asked.

'About what?'

'A new start. I want to do everything right this time,' Dawn explained.

'I don't know …' Ryan started to say.

'Just think about it, OK?' Dawn said.

***

Seth and Kirsten were sitting outside when Ryan and Dawn returned. They were laughing. Kirsten was surprised. She'd never seen Ryan laugh before.

'We should probably leave soon,' Dawn said.

Seth glared at Kirsten. He didn't want them to go.

'I was thinking …' Kirsten started. 'You've just arrived and you don't have anywhere to stay. Why don't you stay here?'

'And there's a party tonight,' Seth added. 'Vegas Night.'

'Another Newport party? Is that a good idea?' Ryan wondered.

'It's nice of you to offer, but I haven't got anything to wear.' Dawn had noticed that Ryan didn't look happy.

'Oh, that's no problem. I can find you something,' Kirsten replied.

***

'It's a Newport charity night, so Summer will be there. I was thinking, Ryan, maybe I should tell her about Tahiti?' Seth looked at Ryan.

'Tahiti? Summer doesn't know you yet. And you want to tell her about your secret plan to take her to Tahiti on a boat?' Ryan asked.

'OK, maybe not the *whole* plan. Just a few details. Play a little game. Girls like games, right?' Seth continued. 'I could leave Summer a note.'

Seth was still talking, but Ryan wasn't listening. He was looking at himself in the mirror. He wasn't used to wearing a suit. And he was worried about the party, about his mom, and about Marissa and Luke …

'Maybe we should just take it quietly tonight. At least, I should. I don't want any more trouble,' Ryan said.

'Right … I see. Keep Tahiti a surprise. That's good thinking.' Seth smiled.

***

Ryan and Dawn walked into the room together. It looked exactly like one of the best casinos in Las Vegas.

'Are all their parties like this?' Dawn asked in surprise.

'Yeah,' Ryan said.

'Well, let's go and win some money!' Dawn laughed and took Ryan over to a blackjack* table.

'Hey, don't worry! It's for charity.' Dawn had seen Ryan's worried face. 'Anyway, I plan to win!'

A guy at the table screamed 'Blackjack!' and the crowd around the table went crazy.

Dawn won almost immediately. 'See? Our luck's changed!' she cried.

Ryan smiled. This was the mom that he remembered. For the first time in months, Ryan felt lucky.

***

Across the room, Seth was with Summer at a craps* table.

'Do it again. You bring me good luck!' Summer held out her hand and Seth blew on the dice.

Summer won again. She took Seth's arm and laughed. 'You're not going anywhere, Syd.'

'Seth,' he corrected her.

But Summer wasn't listening. She held out the dice. 'Blow,' she ordered. And she won again.

'If this goes on,' thought Seth, 'we'll soon be in Tahiti.'

***

Marissa was watching her parents. They weren't talking. 'Does Mom know about the money that Dad's borrowed from Kirsten?' she wondered. 'And why is Dad so quiet?' She looked up and saw Ryan.

Dawn noticed Marissa looking at Ryan. 'Hey, go and have fun with your friends,' she said.

'Sure?' Ryan asked.

'I'll be fine.' Dawn smiled, but her hands shook.

* Blackjack and craps are casino games.

Ryan walked over to Marissa. 'Hey,' he said.

'Hi … Is that your mom?' she asked.

'Yeah,' Ryan said slowly. Usually he was too embarrassed to tell people.

'So I guess you're going home?' Marissa said.

Ryan looked at his mom. 'Yeah. I guess.'

'Well, good luck … with everything,' Marissa said. She was thinking about the night in the model home.

'Yeah. You too,' Ryan looked away. This was too hard. He saw Luke looking at them. 'You should go.'

***

At the blackjack table, Dawn's hands were still shaking.

'I can't do this,' she thought. 'I can't be the perfect mom.' She ordered a drink.

***

Marissa slowly walked over to Luke. 'You can't just ignore me,' she said.

'Watch me,' Luke replied and left.

Marissa followed. 'It was your fault, too. You wanted a fight.'

'You left *me* and went to see *him*,' Luke shouted angrily.

'It wasn't like that ...' Marissa began, but Luke walked past her. Marissa sat alone and upset. Now she had lost both Ryan *and* Luke.

Ryan saw what had happened. 'Hey, Luke,' he called.

'What do you want?' Luke glared at him.

'Nothing happened ... with me and Marissa. She chose *you*,' Ryan lied. 'You're the one she wants.' And then he walked away.

Luke found Marissa sitting alone. He kissed her.

'Sorry,' he said.

***

Seth and Summer were still winning at craps.

'You're fantastic, Stanley!' Summer said and hugged Seth.

He was having fun ... even if Summer didn't know his name.

***

Everyone was having a good time. Ryan tried to enjoy himself, but he felt very alone. Suddenly there was a loud crash.

'Mom!' Ryan ran over. Dawn was lying on the floor with broken glass all around her.

Ryan was embarrassed and angry – everyone was looking.

'What are you looking at?' Dawn shouted. 'Help me up!' She was drunk.

Ryan couldn't move. Seth and Luke arrived and helped Dawn stand up.

'Where's Ryan? Ryan!' Dawn screamed.

Ryan couldn't pretend it wasn't happening any more.

'Mom,' he said quietly as she put her arm around his shoulder.

'I'm sorry, Ryan … do you hate me?' Dawn was crying now.

Ryan wanted to say yes, but he couldn't. He wanted a family. 'No, Mom … I love you.'

***

Ryan sat on his bed and watched his mom sleep.

'It's always going to be like this,' he thought. 'I'll never have a normal family. Why do I always have to take care of everyone? When will someone take care of me?'

***

When Ryan woke up, his mom had disappeared. He went outside and saw her talking to Kirsten. Ryan saw the bag in Dawn's hand. She was trying to leave without saying goodbye. She saw Ryan and waved. Just one wave and she walked away. Ryan knew she was never coming back.

CHAPTER 6
'Two handsome young men ...'

'Dude. You're a Cohen now!' Seth cried.

Ryan smiled. Sandy and Kirsten had decided to become his guardians. Finally, he had a home and a family.

'Now that you're a Cohen,' Seth continued, 'there's a few things you should know. Mom can't cook. If you see her anywhere near the cooker, you tell me. And don't talk to Dad about musicals ... he'll sing *all* the songs for you!'

They were still laughing when Kirsten came into the pool house.

'What's so funny?' she asked.

The boys just went on laughing. Kirsten looked round the room.

'Right ...' she said. 'We need to go shopping.'

'I've got everything I need ... really,' Ryan said.

'Have you got a tuxedo? Because you're going to need one.'

'What for?'

'For Cotillion*,' Kirsten replied.

'What's Cotillion?' Ryan didn't understand.

'Do you really want to know?' Seth said.

'It's the debutante* dance,' Kirsten explained. '*The* biggest night in Newport.'

'Maybe I shouldn't go,' Ryan said.

'We have to go every year. And now you're part of the family, you have to go too!' Kirsten laughed. 'Come on. Let's find you a tuxedo. It'll be fun.'

Kirsten drove the boys to the Country Club. They walked inside and followed her into a large room. It was full of long, white dresses and tuxedos.

---

* Cotillion is a dance where young women (the debutantes) are introduced to society.

Ryan finally found a tuxedo that fitted and went to look in the mirror. 'Life here isn't so bad,' he thought.

'Hey, what are you doing here?' It was Marissa. 'I thought you were leaving … with your mom.'

Ryan was embarrassed. 'Things have changed … so I'm living with the Cohens now.'

'You're really staying?' she asked.

'Yeah. If I can stay away from trouble,' Ryan answered.

'Wow. So we're neighbours …' Marissa finally said.

'Is that OK?' Ryan wasn't sure how Marissa felt.

'No, it's not OK,' Marissa said. 'It's great! We can be friends, right?'

'Friends? That's better than nothing, I guess,' Ryan thought. 'Yeah. Friends – that's cool,' he said.

They both smiled.

Just then, Luke arrived. 'What are you still doing here? I thought you went back to Chino.'

'Change of plan,' Ryan said.

'Ryan's living here now,' Marissa explained and stepped between them.

'*What*?' said Luke.

'Look, I don't want any trouble,' Ryan said.

'Then stay away from me. And stay away from Marissa,' Luke said angrily and walked out.

'Ah, Marissa,' Kirsten came over. 'You're the lead deb* this year, aren't you? These two handsome young men would like to offer their help!' She pointed to Seth and Ryan. 'If any of your girls don't have a partner …'

Summer came over. 'Every girl needs a partner,' she said. She was looking at Ryan.

Seth didn't notice. 'Seth Cohen, here to help,' he said to Summer.

---

* The lead deb (debutante) is the girl who organises the dance.

But Summer ignored him. 'So you'll be at the practice?' She was still looking at Ryan.

'Sure,' said Seth.

***

Summer and Marissa were trying on dresses.

'That Chino guy's back. He looks a bit lonely,' Summer said. 'And you're the lead deb so I was thinking …'

'You want Ryan as a partner?' Marissa asked. 'But you said he was crazy.'

'I didn't know him then,' said Summer.

'And you know him now?'

'I've just met him. Anyway, he looks like a bad boy. I can save him,' Summer smiled.

'Have you talked to him? He's not really a bad boy,' Marissa said. She wanted to be the girl to save Ryan. The only girl who understood him.

'Oh, he will be, when he's with me!' Summer laughed. Then she saw Marissa's face. 'What? You don't like him, do you? You're with Luke, right?'

'Right,' Marissa said, but she wasn't happy about the idea.

CHAPTER 7
Dancing, not fighting

'I don't dance.'

Ryan and Seth were outside the ballroom. It was practice day.

'Come on. Summer will be there and I need you to be there too,' Seth said, and walked in. Ryan followed.

'So, guys, can I introduce you to your debs?' said Marissa.

Summer came over. 'We've already met.'

'Summer, I've promised Ryan to someone else,' Marissa said.

'What? I can't believe you gave him to someone else. Who? Who hasn't got a partner for Cotillion yet?'

'At this moment, that would be you,' a voice said.

Summer turned round. She saw a girl with brown eyes and short, blond hair. She was beautiful and had a style all of her own.

Marissa introduced her. 'Anna Stern, this is Ryan Atwood. Anna's just moved here from Pittsburg.'

'Pittsburg?' Summer was angry.

But Anna just took Ryan's arm and walked away. 'Let's just go,' she said.

Seth stood quietly behind Summer, waiting for her to notice him. Finally Summer turned to him.

'OK. Just don't talk to me.'

Seth smiled. 'Because we don't need words, do we?' he said.

Summer glared at him.

'Right. Understood. No talking,' Seth said quickly.

On the dance floor, Marissa was trying to teach Anna and Ryan how to waltz*.

---

* A waltz is a type of dance.

'No … not like that. Here, watch.' Marissa stepped into Anna's place.

Marissa and Ryan made a good couple and the room seemed to go silent.

A voice said, 'I'd be jealous if Chino was a *real* man.' It was Luke.

Ryan went back to Anna.

'So you like her?' Anna asked.

Ryan was surprised. How did she know?

'I guess that means you're in trouble,' she added.

'I know,' Ryan said.

This could never end well.

* * *

When they got back to the pool house, Seth was really happy.

'Ryan, did you see us dancing?' Seth couldn't stop thinking about Summer. They'd spent all afternoon dancing together *and* she'd told him that he wasn't too bad.

'Yeah,' Ryan laughed.

'I've got a plan,' Seth said.

'What now?' Ryan thought. He didn't want any more trouble. He just wanted to enjoy having a home and a family.

'OK … Things are going well with Summer, but I need to see her again before tomorrow.' Seth looked at Ryan. Ryan didn't look happy. 'And you need a plan too. Anna seems pretty cool. And she's new in Newport. Maybe you two will … you know … Or she might make Marissa jealous …'

'Yeah, right,' Ryan said. He didn't want to make Marissa jealous. They'd agreed to be friends.

Seth got up to leave. 'Oh … and Holly's having another party at her beach house. We need to go. So I can talk to Summer.'

'No!' said Ryan, but Seth had already left.

***

'A Newport beach party … Kids drinking … There won't be any trouble here,' Ryan joked as they walked into Holly's house.

'Ten minutes,' Seth promised as he disappeared to look for Summer.

Ryan sat down. And then he saw Marissa, standing with Luke and his friends. She looked really bored. He wanted to run over and rescue her, but he couldn't. Then Marissa saw Ryan and waved. Ryan shook his head, but Marissa still came over.

Outside, Summer was talking to Holly. 'Cohen's a good dancer. Why don't you go to Cotillion with him, and I'll go with your partner?' she suggested. But Holly didn't want to change.

'Hello, Summer,' Seth said as he walked towards the two girls.

'What did I say about talking to me?' she said quickly.

'Yeah, I know. I just wanted to check everything was OK for tomorrow,' Seth replied.

'I guess …' Summer knew she didn't have any choice.

'Could you just *pretend* to be a bit happy about it?' Seth asked.

Summer glared at him.

'Right,' he said and walked away. 'Soon we'll be in Tahiti and we'll forget about all of this,' he thought.

Back inside, Marissa sat down next to Ryan.

'I'm glad you came,' she said.

'Really?' Ryan was surprised.

'Yeah … how could you possibly miss all this?' Marissa laughed and looked round the room.

'Yeah, right.' Ryan saw Luke coming over and stood up. He knew this was bad news.

'I see you're having fun,' Luke said.

Ryan said nothing. Marissa tried to hold Luke back.

'We're just friends,' she said, but Luke ignored her.

'There are all these people here,' Luke said, 'but you only want to talk to Marissa. Why?'

'*I* wanted to talk to *him*,' Marissa said. She was surprised at herself. She didn't usually stand up to Luke like this.

'Look, Marissa, why don't you go and talk to Summer? She's on her own,' Luke said.

But Marissa didn't want to go. She wanted to finish talking to Ryan. She didn't care what Luke wanted.

'That's OK ... I'm just going,' Ryan stepped back.

'No, stay!' Marissa said.

Luke stepped between them. 'What are you doing? Don't tell him he can stay,' he said angrily.

Ryan couldn't stop himself. 'Don't tell her what to do,' he said.

'I thought you were leaving. Here, let me help you.' Luke pushed Ryan towards the door.

'I'm not going to fight,' Ryan said.

'Oh yeah? Even if I do this?' Luke hit Ryan in the stomach and Ryan fell on the floor.

Ryan wanted to hit Luke, but he couldn't. He'd promised Sandy and Kirsten that there'd be no more fights.

Marissa left angrily and Luke followed her.

'Hey, Luke hit you and you didn't fight back. You really are a Cohen,' Seth joked as he helped Ryan off the floor.

Ryan didn't smile. 'I've got a home and a family now, but I didn't think it would be this hard,' he thought. He looked at Seth and for the first time he completely understood how he felt. Living somewhere and still not being a part of it. And one thing was certain – he knew he couldn't go to Cotillion.

CHAPTER 8
Dance partners

Ryan sat on his bed reading comics. His tuxedo was hanging up.

'Why aren't you dressed?' Seth asked as he walked into the pool house.

'I'm not going,' Ryan said. 'Could you tell Anna? She'll probably be pleased.'

***

Marissa sat on her bed looking at her white dress. Cotillion was in two hours, but she didn't want to go. Julie walked into the room, but she didn't notice her daughter's sad face.

'I love your dress,' Julie said.

'Maybe *you* should wear it,' Marissa said.

'That's sweet, but we both know it won't fit me,' Julie laughed.

'I don't think I want to go.' Marissa looked at her mom.

'What?'

'Luke and I had a fight last night, OK?' Marissa said.

'So you had a fight. You've had fights before,' Julie replied. 'You two have been together for years.'

'Maybe that's the problem,' Marissa said. 'What if there's someone else?'

Julie looked at Marissa. 'Who? That boy from Chino?'

Marissa didn't answer.

'Do you want to be like your aunt Cindy? Poor, with four kids?' Julie said. 'She broke my mom's heart, and I won't let you break mine.'

'Oh, so this is all about you,' Marissa said angrily.

'No, it's about you. What kind of future can that boy

offer you?'

'Mom, I'm sixteen …' Marissa cried.

'Yes,' Julie replied, 'and the choices that you make when you're sixteen are important. Luke comes from a good family. If you stay with him, you will always be comfortable.'

But Marissa didn't want to be comfortable. She wanted to be free, to feel excited again.

'Nothing in life is certain,' Julie said angrily.

'What do you mean?' Marissa asked. She guessed her mom wasn't only talking about her and Luke.

'I mean, you're going to put on that dress and go to Cotillion with Luke,' was all Julie said.

'No.' Marissa knew that if Luke was her partner for Cotillion, it would be Marissa and Luke forever. 'I'm sorry.'

'No, you're not. But you will be.' Julie left the room angrily.

***

'Anna! Anna? Has anyone seen …' Seth shouted.

'Seth, behind you,' Anna said.

Seth turned round and saw Anna in her Cotillion dress. She looked amazing.

'Wow!' was all he could say.

'Do you think so?' Anna didn't sound sure.

'Yeah. And that makes this more difficult to say …'

'Ryan's not coming,'

Anna finished for him.

'Yeah. Are you OK?' Seth was worried.

'Sure. I'll survive,' Anna said and kicked her shoes off.

Seth watched her go. He liked her style.

***

At the Cohens' house, Ryan was showing Sandy a new PlayStation game. He was glad he hadn't gone to Cotillion.

'You didn't feel like going, huh?' Sandy asked.

'No … not really for me,' Ryan answered. He thought about Marissa in her dress.

'What? Dancing and flowers not your style?' Sandy joked.

Ryan smiled.

'You know … everyone at Cotillion feels the same. They've all got secrets and they're all afraid that someone's going to find out.'

Ryan thought about the secrets he already knew. Luke cheating on Marissa. Marissa's dad. 'So what's your secret?' he asked Sandy.

'Sometimes, early in the morning, when the surf's good and when Kirsten isn't angry with me … I quite like this place.'

Ryan smiled. He was starting to like this place too.

***

There was a knock at the door. Ryan opened it.

'Summer told me you weren't at Cotillion,' said Marissa.

'You didn't go either?' Ryan said in surprise.

She followed him into the kitchen.

'Hiding at home isn't going to make everything better,'

he said to Marissa.

'You're doing it too!' she replied quickly.

Ryan smiled.

'I'll go if you go,' Marissa offered.

'I can't hide forever,' Ryan thought. 'OK,' he said.

***

'I don't believe it!' Julie shouted when Marissa and Ryan walked into the Country Club.

But Luke wasn't happy. 'You told Summer you weren't coming. And now you're here with *him*?'

'I'm not ... Ryan and I aren't ...' Marissa tried to explain.

'I'm not stupid. We're finished,' Luke said and left angrily.

Ryan didn't know what to do. He stood in a corner while Marissa and her mom talked.

'Well, you can't dance without a partner,' Julie finally said.

Ryan walked over to them. 'If you need a partner ...' he said to Marissa.

'It's nice of you to offer, but no thanks,' Julie said.

Marissa smiled at Ryan. 'I'll get dressed,' she said.

CHAPTER 9
The debutante dance

'Look at you ...' Anna said as she walked up to Seth. 'A lonely guy sitting on the floor, feeling sorry for himself. Sad!'

Seth was sitting on the floor outside the ballroom. Summer had found another partner and he was feeling terrible. He turned to Anna.

'Yeah, right ... you're not making me feel any better,' he said.

Anna sat down next to him. 'You know what your problem is? You're not a man.'

'Right ... now I feel *much* better,' Seth said unhappily.

But Anna wasn't trying to hurt Seth. She liked him and she was trying to help.

'Do you know what girls like ... what they find attractive?' she asked.

'Guys who play water polo, like Luke?' Seth asked. He wasn't sure what Anna meant.

'You know what else?' she asked.

'No,' Seth said.

'Guys who are confident. Watch this.' She sat down next to Seth. 'Hey, Seth, I don't have a partner for Cotillion. Do you want to go with me?'

Suddenly Seth didn't know what to do. No girl had ever invited him to anything before. Most girls just ignored him. Anna moved a little closer.

'Be a man, Cohen!'

Seth stood up and offered her his arm. He liked her. She made him feel like a new man. Confident. They walked back to the ballroom together.

When they got there, Summer came up to Seth.

'Listen, you can be my partner again,' she said.

'Sorry, I've already got a partner,' Seth said. He looked at Anna and smiled. He'd said no to Summer. He didn't need Summer, he had Anna.

***

'Good evening. Welcome to the forty-seventh Newport Beach Debutante Cotillion …'

Ryan and Marissa walked out of the dressing rooms.

'Are you ready?' Marissa asked.

Ryan looked at her. She looked so beautiful. 'Yes,' he said quietly. With Marissa by his side, he felt that anything was possible.

Soft music played in the hall. There were white flowers everywhere. One by one, the Newport girls walked into the room with their fathers and were introduced to the guests. Then each father led his daughter to her partner.

The first dance began. Ryan put his arm around Marissa and they danced. Next to them, Seth danced with Anna. Seth and Ryan had found their partners. They both smiled.

Ryan looked into Marissa's eyes and held her close.

'Maybe some day we can be more than just friends,' he thought.

Marissa looked at Ryan and at all the people around them.

'Everything will be OK if Ryan is here,' she thought. 'Tonight is perfect. I know Luke left me, but I'm OK. And I finally stood up to Mom. I can finally be me.'

Suddenly there was a lot of shouting. It was Holly's dad, Greg Fisher, and he was shouting at Jimmy. People started looking at them. Soon, a crowd of people were standing around them. Marissa heard the noise and turned round to look. She was just in time to see Greg Fisher hit her dad. Hard. Jimmy fell to the floor. He was unconscious.

Marissa ran to her dad. She sat down next to him and held his head.

'Dad,' she cried softly. 'That's what you've been hiding. Why won't you talk to me?'

'Whatever the problem is, it isn't just borrowing money from Kirsten. It's bigger than that,' Marissa thought. She started crying. She wanted to go back to when she was a little girl and her dad seemed perfect.

The doctors arrived. Marissa looked at her dad once more and then ran out of the room. Ryan watched Marissa disappear. He wanted to follow her. But he knew she needed time alone.

Seth came over. 'Hey, is it OK if I walk home with Anna? I know she was your partner, but …' he asked Ryan.

'No, sure. I'll see you at home,' Ryan replied and walked towards the door.

'See you at home,' Seth repeated. 'That sounds good,' he thought happily. 'We both live there now.'

***

Seth walked over to Anna and offered her his arm.

'So do you think I'll see you again?' he asked. He liked Anna. Sure, he still liked Summer and still wanted to take her to Tahiti. His plans hadn't changed, but Anna was special. Another person who could be a real friend – he didn't want to lose her.

'No,' she replied quickly.

'Oh. OK,' Seth said in surprise. He thought the night had gone well.

'I know this sounds kind of strange … But I'm going sailing for the rest of the summer … to Tahiti,' Anna explained.

Seth was stunned. *Tahiti*? This girl was perfect. And they left, both smiling.

✳✳✳

Ryan found Marissa outside. She was crying.

'Are you OK?' he asked.

Marissa shook her head. 'What happened in there?' she asked.

'I don't know.' There was nothing Ryan could say to help.

'What's going to happen now?' Marissa whispered.

'I don't know.' Ryan put his jacket around her. He knew what it was like to feel totally alone. To feel that your world has changed forever. He held her tight.

'Come on. Let's go,' he said. They started to walk back. Marissa tried to smile, but she couldn't.

Suddenly Luke stood in front of them. He wanted to help, but Marissa didn't want to speak to him. She didn't want another fight between Ryan and Luke. She didn't want to have to choose between them. She needed to be alone.

Marissa handed Ryan his jacket and walked away, leaving him and Luke together. Then she took off her shoes and started to run across the grass. Finally she threw herself onto the ground. The tears were falling down her face. She thought about her dad lying unconscious on the floor.

'What's going to happen now?' Marissa wondered. 'Will things *ever* be the same again?'

FACT FILE

On set with

THE OC™

It's a top TV show and is now in its third series. The beaches are beautiful, the people are beautiful and the parties are wild! So what happens on set on the coolest TV show around?

Forget the sunscreen!

Most of *The OC* is filmed inside in a specially designed set. As we know, in *The OC* the sun always shines but real life California does have cloudy days. By filming inside, the crew don't have to worry about the weather – they make their own weather with special lights and equipment.

Working and chilling

It takes five to seven days to film just one episode of *The OC*. The actors work from between six to sixteen hours a day. Each actor has their own dressing room. They go there when they're not filming.

'It's really funny,' says Adam, 'Each room has a sofa, a phone and a small table but the girls' rooms are really different to the guys'. The girls' rooms are like bedrooms – they've got candles, and posters on the walls. My room hasn't got anything like that in it!'

All of the actors love to listen to

What do these words mean? You can use a dictionary.

(on) set   series   crew   chill   episode   frog   gross

music in their rooms. Ben likes country music and Rachel plays hip-hop. Mischa's a *Radiohead* fan and Adam likes indie bands. Chris plays his own music on his guitar.

Birthdays and dead frogs!

The OC stars are all good friends, and enjoy having fun together. Adam is the joker of the group.

'We always remember birthdays and we buy cakes and presents,' says Mischa. 'When it was Rachel's birthday, we were filming in the school biology room. We were cutting up dead frogs. Rachel had lots of presents in her dressing room and Adam put one of the dead frogs into a box. It looked like a present. So, Rachel went home and opened her presents and there was the dead frog! It was gross! Rachel called me and she was screaming, 'We've got to do something to Adam!' She knew it was him!

Who's who?
Ryan: Ben McKenzie
Marissa: Mischa Barton
Seth: Adam Brody
Summer: Rachel Bilson
Luke: Chris Carmack

The Kiss

There's lots of kissing in *The OC* but what's it like for the actors?

'Kissing someone for a job is strange,' says Ben. 'It's not romantic at all! There are usually about 100 people watching you. You have to forget that they're there.'

Do you watch *The OC*? What do you like or dislike about it?

FACT FILE

Mischa Barton

Marissa Cooper seems to have it all. She wears designer clothes, goes to the coolest parties and everyone loves her. But she also drinks too much and is in love with Chino bad boy Ryan Atwood. We asked actor Mischa Barton to tell us more about Marissa – and herself.

What do these words mean? You can use a dictionary.
outsider   chill out

What do you think of Marissa?
Marissa is more than just a rich girl. At the start of *The OC*, she's beginning to realise that she doesn't want the usual Newport life. She feels different from people around her. Ryan is very attractive to her because he comes from another world. They are both outsiders in different ways, and that brings them together.

Do you enjoy playing Marissa?
It's great! We are similar in lots of ways. We both like the same designers, we like doing the same things and we both like punk music! We even like the same kind of men – dark and difficult!

How long have you been acting?
Since I was nine. I went to a special acting school so that I could study and have time to act. When I was eleven, I got a small part in *The Sixth Sense* with Bruce Willis. The movie was really successful and after that I got quite a lot of TV and film work.

When did you get *The OC* part?
When I was 17 – the same age as Marissa! I was planning to go to university somewhere and then they offered me the part. I still want to go to university – it's very important to me.

How do you chill out?
When I'm back in New York, I love to go sock shopping with my sister, Hania. I love socks! I've got lots of them! And one of my favourite things is going to see a band. I really like *The Strokes*, *U2* and *Coldplay*.

So you want to be a star? Mischa says ...

⭐ 1 **Believe in yourself.** If you really want to act and you know you can, you'll be successful.

⭐ 2 **Be ready for hard work!** Acting is hard work and the hours can be long. If you really enjoy it, you won't care.

⭐ 3 **Work hard at school.** Acting isn't the only thing in life. Don't leave school because you want to act. You might want to do other things in the future.

> **Would you like to work in the TV or music business?**
> **What qualities do you need?**

FACT FILE

Debutante

In **The OC**, *the Cotillion debutante ball was a very important time for Marissa and her friends. But where does this tradition come from and does it really happen today?*

What does 'cotillion' mean?

🇫🇷 'Cotillion' is a type of dance which was popular in 18th and 19th century France.

Where did debutante balls begin?

🇬🇧 Debutante balls started in the UK in the 18th century. Young girls from rich, upper-class families were introduced to the king or queen of England at court. A 'social season' of dances, parties, dinners and sporting events followed. Every debutante (and her mother!) hoped that she would find a husband by the end of the season.

Entering society wasn't only for the upper classes. Girls from middle-class families were also introduced to society. There was usually a ball or a party to celebrate. After a girl was 'out', she was invited to dinners and balls but always with her parents or an older married family friend.

What happens now?

In 1958, Queen Elizabeth II stopped the presenting of debutantes at court. The social season, however, is still a part of British life today. It starts in April and runs until the end of October. It includes events in and around the London area such as the Ascot races and the Henley Regatta. Today anyone can buy tickets for these events.

Fun at the Ascot races

What do these words mean? You can use a dictionary.

ball   tradition/traditional   upper/middle-class   court
event   doll   high-heeled

Balls

What happens in other parts of the world?

Latin America

In some Latin American countries, there is a big celebration for a girl's fifteenth birthday. This is called the *quinceañera*. It used to mean that a girl was ready to marry.

Quinceañera celebrations depend on the country and family but there is always some kind of party. Sometimes, the girl is given a *quince* doll. She throws this to the children at the party to show that she is no longer a child.

The girl may wear trainers to the party. After the first dance, the father takes off her trainers, and replaces them with high-heeled shoes. His daughter has become a young lady …

Today, not everyone has a traditional party. Some girls receive a special present, such as a holiday or a car.

Australia and Ireland

In Australia and Ireland, a lot of schools have debutante balls for their older students. Students dress in their best clothes and go with friends or a boyfriend or girlfriend. Often these 'deb balls' are seen as a lot of fun, and no longer a serious tradition.

The USA

There are about forty debutante balls in the US every year, including the Debutante Cotillion in Newport Beach. They are very expensive events, and the money from ticket sales goes to charity. Most American teenagers don't go to Cotillion – high school dances or proms are much more popular.

A Cuban girl celebrates her *quinceañera*

Discussion: What do you think of traditions such as debutante balls, and the *quinceañera*? Are they still important in our society today?

SELF-STUDY ACTIVITIES

CHAPTERS 1–2

Before you read

1 Complete the sentences with these words. Use the correct tense of the verbs. You can use a dictionary.

**attorney   cheat on   get drunk   guardian
probation   water polo**

a) There was a lot of wine at the party and they … .

b) He stole some money, but he didn't go to prison. He got six months' … .

c) I've just started playing … . It's a great team sport.

d) I think Sue's … her boyfriend. I've seen her with another guy.

e) An … gives advice on the law .

f) My parents are dead and I live with my aunt. She's my … .

2 Match each word with its definition. You can use a dictionary.

diner   embarrassed   pier   stunned   suspicious

a) being extremely surprised

b) a place where you can eat cheaply or have a drink

c) thinking someone isn't what they seem

d) a wooden platform that goes from the beach out into the sea

e) feeling nervous or uncomfortable when talking to people

3 Read 'People and Places' on pages 4–5. Who do you think has the most interesting secrets?

After you read

4 Complete the sentences with the correct name. You will need to use some names more than once.

Jimmy   Luke   Marissa   Ryan   Sandy   Seth   Summer   Trey

a) … is in prison.

b) … tries to find Ryan a room in a group home.

c) … takes Ryan to stay in his mom's model home.

d) … becomes friends with Ryan and Seth.

e) … hits Luke in the diner.

f) … asks Kirsten to lend him $100,000.

g) … asks Marissa why she's been acting strangely.

h) … decides to run away because he doesn't want to live in a group home.

i) … doesn't like Ryan.

j) … discovers he likes the same music and books as Marissa.

CHAPTERS 3–5

Before you read

5 Complete the sentences with the correct tense of each verb. You can use a dictionary.

glare   handcuff   hug   ignore

  a) He said hello, but I didn't want to speak to him, so I … him.
  b) Mark was really angry and he … at me.
  c) The police officer … the criminal.
  d) Sally … her boyfriend and then he kissed her.

6 Match the sentence beginnings and endings.

  a) The electricity isn't working – let's light
  b) I want to go camping, but I haven't got
  c) To play the game, throw
  d) The robber hit me on the head and I fell down
  e) All the money from

  i) the dice. Then move the number of spaces on the dice.
  ii) a candle. Then we'll be able to see.
  iii) the charity show is for poor children.
  iv) a sleeping bag. Can you lend me one?
  v) unconscious. I can't remember anything else.

7 What do you think?

  a) Will Ryan move to Austin?
  b) Will Seth, Ryan and Marissa stay friends?

After you read

8 Are the sentences true or false? Correct the false sentences.

  a) The fire starts in the model home when Luke and Ryan are fighting.
  b) Luke leaves Ryan in the model home.
  c) After the fire, Ryan and Luke run away.
  d) Ryan tells Seth about Marissa's visit to the model home.
  e) Julie is pleased to meet Ryan.
  f) Ryan is really happy to see his mom again.
  g) Dawn and her boyfriend are still together.
  h) Ryan lies to Luke about Marissa.

9 What do you think? Write words to describe …

  a) Luke   **b)** Ryan   **c)** Marissa   **d)** Seth

SELF-STUDY ACTIVITIES

CHAPTERS 6–9

Before you read

10 Complete the sentences with these words. You can use a dictionary.

**ballroom   gamble   jealous   musical   society
stands up to   tuxedo**

  a) The formal dance was in the … . All the men had to wear a … .
  b) We went to the theatre to see a … . The story was good, but the songs were terrible!
  c) He was very … when he saw his girlfriend talking to another boy.
  d) Her boyfriend always tells her what to do. She never … him.
  e) In our … , many people think money and success are necessary to be happy.
  f) Paula is starting her own business. It's a bit of a … – let's hope she's successful.

11 What do you think?
  a) What will happen to Ryan now? Will he stay with the Cohens?
  b) Will Summer become friends with Seth?
  c) Will Marissa and Luke stay together?

After you read

12 Answer the questions.
  a) Who does Summer want to go to Cotillion with?
  b) Who does Marissa choose as dance partners for Seth and Ryan?
  c) Why does Seth want to go to Holly's party? Why doesn't Ryan want to go?
  d) What happens at the party?
  e) Why does Julie want Marissa to stay with Luke?
  f) Why do Ryan and Marissa decide to go to Cotillion?
  g) What does Anna tell Seth?
  h) Does Seth like Anna? Why/Why not?

13 What do you think? What will happen to the following characters?
  a) Julie and Jimmy   **b)** Marissa and Ryan   **c)** Anna and Seth